Your consciousness is by far, the greatest exploration you shall ever endeavor to explore.

POP on TOP

EDUCIBLE

This little book is dedicated to YOU!

writ & illustrated by Kea

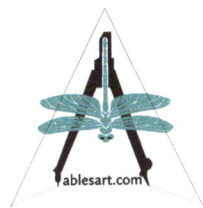

Pop on Top: Educible

© 2023 by Kea Ables

Library of Congress Control Number: 2023917325

ISBN: 979-8-9869195-8-4 Hardcover
ISBN: 979-8-9869195-0-8 Paperback
ISBN: 979-8-9869195-1-5 eBook

First Edition

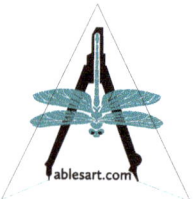
ablesart.com

A continuum
message reaching
far and **wide,**

Reigning within
and throughout
ocean's tide.

POP's message blows
throughout space
beyond conceptual time,

Effects you think
you experience
but cannot find.

Features

Within the
Delicious
Vessel
You are

Create
Paradise 28

On Our Cover

Harvest Issue

87

Get The Word Out

Within the Infinite
Unified Field
What are we choosing to
create today?

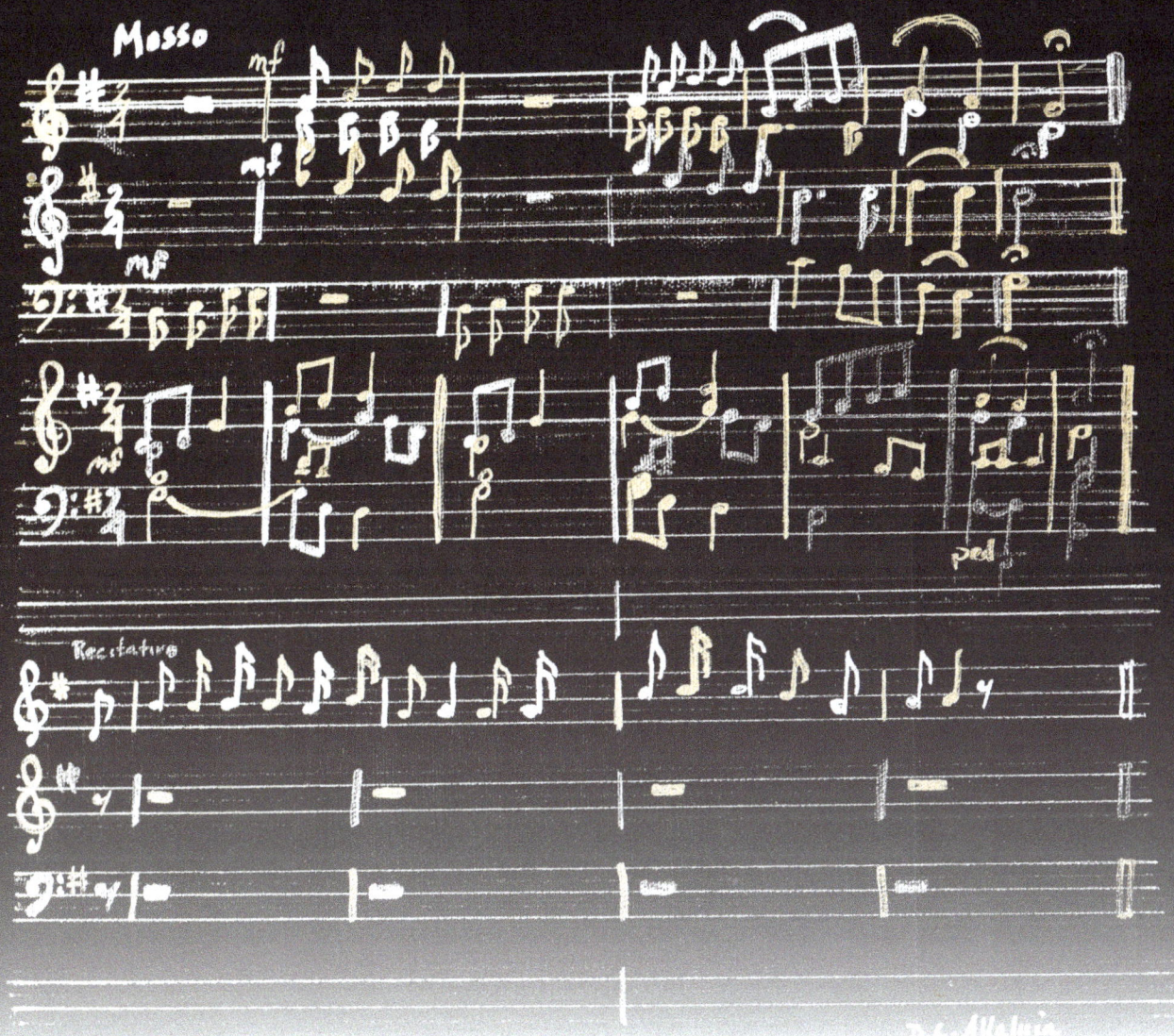

POP wants you to know,
I AM in all things
I'm in newspapers
in movies, In music I sing.

It's not in the **words**

It's not what is **said,**

It's in the space
in-between within the
mystery unread.

Sometimes I AM subtle
even silent to some,

Through the
darkest of nights
when you think you're alone,

I AM a constant
fore **your heart**
is my home.

So breathe the breath
that I AM because it's
incredibly good,

What am I
you ask
I want
you to know,

My message is

Love

and I'd like
it to grow!

for they are
the ones that
widen the way
for our hearts
to grow bigger
and BIGGER each day!

Aquaponics
Gardens
Orchards
Barns

I will you to feel
this **LOVE** so dear,
become it and
share it
Know no fear.

When you choose to remember
you are ONE with POP
holy infinity nothing can stop.

The mirrored
reflection
the image you are
is the face of POP
and YOU
are the star!

May Your Love
Blaze Brightly
Illuminating
Your Path

About the Author & Illustrator

Kea has been an artist her whole life.
From sculpting her hips to commissioned paintings.
Her favorite quote being,
"Art is life, Life is art!"
This little book is an ode to language
And the words that give us wings!

Find out more about Kea and her artwork
at AblesArt.com

Leave a Review!

If you got educibled, please say it out loud.

And share the love.

Thank you!

From my heart to yours.

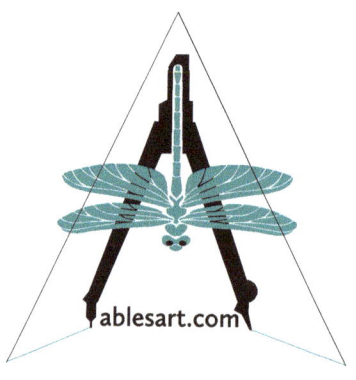

www.ingramcontent.com/pod-product-compliance
Lightning Source LLC
Chambersburg PA
CBHW041543120626
46551CB00019B/2821